This is Jack.

This is Mirjana.

They both like to say hi.

They like to make their fingers leap off of cliffs in other words their knees.

Neat.

How can one express in words how nice it is to be in your company?

I can.

sniff *sniff* *sniff*

It could be Mirjana and Jack Doline.

Wouldn't it be nice?

Meowmix. Kibbles and bits and bits and bits. Some guys have all the fun.

+ Tuti. Critter. Critter of the night. Strangers of the night. Da da da da da da.

At that point I accepted that we have cats. I stood, I looked the train came at me, and then I leaped off the tracks.

Today a train hit me in the left leg. I fell on my left leg at MSU, my tailbone.

Biscuits.

I leaped off the track only to cross onto the dirt and rocks. Only to pass the fence, once again into the grass. How annoying. Only moments ago, I feel I could have just grabbed myself that log, wrote on the gravel and pulled grass. That is like annoyance of the mind. What if you write with a stick in the rocky, dirty, gravel?

There is so much a man can tell you, so much he can say, the power remains, my power, my pleasure, my pain. Ooo.

Dedicated to my dad: Oliver Todor Nikolovski.

Listen to the music,

Listen to my heart break,

Listen to the radio.

Biscuits will be fine. I'd like to see you now Mr. Lancaster. Deep down Ingrid, I feel you are the one.

And the confusion sets in.

Notice it's the number 5 again. 1,2,3,4,5?

Song 2 As though time was once as pure as gold.

Song 3 One by one the cars went by,

Two by two the trees swayed high,

Three by three the door slammed my bow,

Four by four the bells hung low,

Five by five the trees went bye bye,

Six by six the stick went kicks,

Seven by seven the door went heaven,

Eight by eight the door went gate,

Nine by nine the trees went bye bye.

From the valley to the mountain,

I will look beyond a fountain,

What I saw was angels flying,

I will look beyond my pain,

Where the path of truth ends,

I will not look dense,

We will find it together,

We won't let it pass by.

The frog got run over by an iron flattener. Now, don't get any ideas. Hello flys'. Everybody in. Bug sits next to Jimmy Fallen on airplane. They make conversation. Let's get this out of the way Ingrid. Jimmy Fallon supposedly, said, we're the underground. Hello underground. No one talks back to the underground. "We won." Dim the lights. Scene 1: a lover of Frank Sinatra, Dim the lights.

Hitler: Have you included me?

Nay

Did you feel this way your whole life?

I did.

Not anymore.

One day I said no.

I exploit myself to help my family make money in Africa.

Nobody loves me.

Bongo.

It never works out-THE NEWS

Noir Movies.

Everyone wants to rejoice.

Everyone wants to kiss those kitten lips.

Everyone wants to kiss those jealous lips.

Everyone wants to rejoice.

Audition 1: Next let's see your jealous lips.

Two pair of legs off of a pair of jealous lips.

To pale to thy kick.

Da Da Da

I've been chasing you since I was a seedling.

Let it go igloo.

Stay back.

The sign says stay back.

Don't make me get my blind mutt after you.

They go by PAWS.

I need one of those dogs to help me see.

Alright, grab a puppy.

Or better yet a mutt.

Don't be why.

Don't.

Don't listen to the reaper.

And fear not you are one.

You are unlawful and sinister.

Dilly this and dilly that

Smithers this and smithers that

We will travel back in time

In do do do time to meat

OUR SAVIOR

Me-not the SAVIOR

Sonnets

We are all students of the SAVIOR

So am I.

Out of my way.

mmmm.

Don't.

Hello!

Hellu!

Retake

Heeluuu!

I've discovered screaming harry!

At age 34.

Shut it.

I said shut it!

I used to steal Nylons and Brownies.

Arrest me.

Even powder for your face.

Beep you.

Beep beep beep beep beep ya.

There's someone I'm longing to see.

Turns out it's me.

Someone to watch over me.

Psycho.

I miss the nudity.

Not like that.

Pouring the sparkles by another.

Silky very sad poetry.

The look on your face when I read the silence.

I miss the fawn nude leap.

I miss the nude dance.

"You look weird in that scene, confused but you look good naked!" –Jin

I wasn't going to write that.

It's times like these you learn to love again.

I don't won't anymore. Aw.

Feel it out. Mr. Operator number nine.

Down by the bank, from bank to banky singin eeeee I o ker plop.

Skip it.

Skip it. Skip it. We're part of your neighborhood.

Puppy Surprise. There could be three or four of five. How many puppies are there inside?

Make it. Don't break it.

The KORS

Why won't you tell me she said. (can't)

Now I'm gonna love you till the heavens are parade.

Now I'm gonna love you (sing it)

Till the stars come out, the stars for you and I.

(.) (.)

(.) (.)

-

–

Don't makea mia saya somethinga.

Translation

Don't make me say something.

Because I ain't sayin it.

I said Oscar, I ain't sayin it.

Dear Brownies

How come I can't have one?

Oh wait, you gave me one thank you.

I remember you didn't make me sell any.

One scuba snack.

Sold for 10. Good!

Scuba Tank.

Tang Top.

A tuba toba.

A happy bear.

Hm.

Ingrid. It's time to show off.

Dear Ingrid,

Seems you didn't make it today.

Or forever for that matter.

Meet me at the Gap.

And I'll be a happy Greeter.

Ingrid, I like the way you look.

I like the way you move.

I like your sense of style.

I also like your long locks and long legs too.

Dear show off,

These are the voices talking.

Don't go there.

Last but not least

You don't have to print this

But what are you to do Ingrid.

If you don't print this, you'll be more than a salmonella lock.

Sincerely,

Your Truly

The Terminator

Peace be with you

May peace be with you I mean

Thursday 2016

Hollywood is an evil government.

Whoops sh.

Does anyone have any Cheerios?

It's like one minute your going straight, then the next minute you fall off a cliff!

Happy Days!

In a panic you don't know where you're going.

1 All criminals rejoice.

Every criminal rejoice.

2 There were engines, Ventura, fire engines.

In a panic, you don't know where you are going.

3 All criminals rejoice

There were engines, fire engines.

She used to chase those cars around like they were wild horses.

We're here for you every morning providing you can afford a TV.

Say it isn't so.

What would you do if you were homeless?

Talk to a stranger.

It's a strange condition.

A day in prison.

Got me out of my head

And I don't know what I came for

Keep me together baby

Turn it all around

I don't know what I came for

Got me together baby

But I know you to know ooo wow.

It's a strange condition.

Ressurection is through the eyes.

"How was the party?"-me, Mirjana

"The party was fun." –Joel Kauffman

KADIMA HALLOWEEN PARTY, BEVERLY HILLS

"How do you know you're not crinkle, if you'r e not crinkle?"-Mr. Lancaster

Medium

Mirjana

The lulu press

"The dream will unite the world"

Remember that everyone?

So I traveled to The Chicago Actors Studio on the train which made my hair nicer and I traveled at the speed of light E=mc2.

Try to remember what your mind won't allow you to forget. "?

-I'll just end up nakid at KFC

With someone pulling my underwear string.

I will watch the weather channel again.

You guys read. Let's go on a train through Europe. Pure imagination.

Pete is York.

Let me see

When I see Jimmy

I see stars

And it's no wonder!

A piece of paper I write on

Disappears.

I see me, in my dream

Meeting Jimmy

& just when I'm about to get there the

Dream disappears.

Though I shook his hand.

I see tears welling

 Up & I see

Someone alone. Me.

I didn't recognize myself.

I was watching myself and I was

Like who is that? Me!

Why is it under Mirjana 2?

Hm?

Mirjana Nikolovski

Novel-Script

Mirjana Nikolovski

Novel-Script

Vampires

Vampires live forever.

They go by the name of James.

Mr. Kitten Kat

Mrs. Kitten Kat

Where is my coughin bar?

Where is my coughin surgery?

"Where is my john Wayne?"

"Where have all the cowboys gone?"

';Ooo

Chicken Tacos

Chicken Cats

Chicken little rockin down the

Street

With Rockadoodle.

Sycamore Street

Bennavile

Sycamore Street

Haven

Presidency

Please take your invitation

Crickets

Sycamore Street

Bennaville Sycamore

Bennaville Sycamore Crickets

Kittens

Kentucky

Flyin Cockroaches Cockroaches on a string

Pets

Lightning Bugs

Three three

Three yet back in time

Car Crash

A wedding ring bends

Soft train

Break it down

Frusterated incorporated

Cross train incorporated

Kids incorporated

AW

Shoes

May we?

May I?

Me, single space

You

Who.

Planetary kids incorporated

Crickets

Snails

Escargot

Why does one get accused?

Wronly of Escargo?

What if it were escargot?

Then say it ain't so.

The End

Scene

Light Fade To Dark

And I'm feeling something now.

You're the only one I ever hold.

If you wanna hold me now.

Gold.

Thank You.

Kids Incorporated.

Woof.

Seldom do we know who we really are...

Seldom do we see anything else.

The dream is that your nakid at KFC.

I mean that like the guy that got arrested for being nakid at KFC.

So it's a crime to be nakid these days!

And yet the garden of Eaden did Infact exist.

It can exist. It hasn't happened yet

Let's make it happen!

Outside!

Allow what your dreams won't allow you to forget.

Criminal behavior

"From this point on I am now a criminal." – cancer

k

Bronz

Pinny Party

Confetti

Treasures of a dream

Nance,

-Facial expressions do-not develop, if people do not look at your face.

-You can always do it with muscle stigmatization.

-Does that get boring?

-In my opinion, yes.

But not, that boring.

[Muscle stigmatization was invented in 1982]

[It is a vibration of the muscles.]

[It is a vibration of the muscle tissue.]

Let me be

Mrs. Understood,

Sincerely,

Mirjana

[For a while, after my accident, I was chased, victimized by my legs.]

[Always| coca |co|la]